# Police and Criminal Evidence Act 1984 (PACE)

# CODE G
## Revised

### CODE OF PRACTICE FOR THE STATUTORY POWER OF ARREST BY POLICE OFFICERS

November 2012

# GRAN*GIS* UK Publishing

Adapted and Published by GRANGIS (Grand Register Library).
Online:  www.grangis.com.
E-mail: contact@grangis.com.

# 1   Introduction

1.1   This Code of Practice deals with the statutory power of police to arrest a person who is involved, or suspected of being involved, in a criminal offence.  The power of arrest must be used fairly, responsibly, with respect for people suspected of committing offences and without unlawful discrimination.  The Equality Act 2010 makes it unlawful for police officers to discriminate against, harass or victimise any person on the grounds of the 'protected characteristics' of age, disability, gender reassignment, race, religion or belief, sex and sexual orientation, marriage and civil partnership, pregnancy and maternity when using their powers.  When police forces are carrying out their functions they also have a duty to have regard to the need to eliminate unlawful discrimination, harassment and victimisation and to take steps to foster good relations.

1.2   The exercise of the power of arrest represents an obvious and significant interference with the Right to Liberty and Security under Article 5 of the European Convention on Human Rights set out in Part I of Schedule 1 to the Human Rights Act 1998.

1.3   The use of the power must be fully justified and officers exercising the power should consider if the necessary objectives can be met by other, less intrusive means.  Absence of justification for exercising the power of arrest may lead to challenges should the case proceed to court.  It could also lead to civil claims against police for unlawful arrest and false imprisonment.  When the power of arrest is exercised it is essential that it is exercised in a non-discriminatory and proportionate manner which is compatible with the Right to Liberty under Article 5.  See *Note 1B*.

1.4   Section 24 of the Police and Criminal Evidence Act 1984 (as substituted by section 110 of the Serious Organised Crime and Police Act 2005) provides the statutory power for a constable to arrest without warrant for all offences.  If the provisions of the Act and this Code are not observed, both the arrest and the conduct of any subsequent investigation may be open to question.

1.5   This Code of Practice must be readily available at all police stations for consultation by police officers and police staff, detained persons and members of the public.

1.6   The *Notes for Guidance* are not provisions of this code.

## 2.   Elements of Arrest under section 24 PACE

2.1   A lawful arrest requires two elements:

A person's involvement or suspected involvement or attempted involvement in the commission of a criminal offence;

**AND**

Reasonable grounds for *believing* that the person's arrest is necessary.

- both elements must be satisfied, and
- it can never be necessary to arrest a person unless there are reasonable grounds to suspect them of committing an offence.

2.2   The arrested person must be informed that they have been arrested, even if this fact is obvious, and of the relevant circumstances of the arrest in relation to both the above elements.  The custody officer must be informed of these matters on arrival at the police station.  See *paragraphs 2.9, 3.3* and *Note 3* and *Code C paragraph 3.4.*

*(a) 'Involvement in the commission of an offence'*

2.3   A constable may arrest without warrant in relation to any offence (see *Notes 1* and *1A*) anyone:

- who is about to commit an offence <u>or</u> is in the act of committing an offence;
- whom the officer has reasonable grounds for suspecting is about to commit an offence <u>or</u> to be committing an offence;
- whom the officer has reasonable grounds to suspect of being guilty of an offence which he or she has reasonable grounds for suspecting has been committed;
- anyone who is guilty of an offence which has been committed or anyone whom the officer has reasonable grounds for suspecting to be guilty of that offence.

2.3A  There must be some reasonable, objective grounds for the suspicion, based on known facts and information which are relevant to the likelihood the offence has been committed and the person liable to arrest committed it. See *Notes 2* and *2A.*

*(b) Necessity criteria*

2.4   The power of arrest is <u>only</u> exercisable if the constable has reasonable grounds for *believing* that it is necessary to arrest the person.  The statutory criteria for what may constitute necessity are set out in paragraph 2.9 and it remains an operational decision at the discretion of the constable to decide:

- which one or more of the necessity criteria (if any) applies to the individual; and
- if any of the criteria do apply, whether to arrest, grant street bail after arrest, report for summons or for charging by post, issue a penalty notice or take any other action that is open to the officer.

2.5   In applying the criteria, the arresting officer has to be satisfied that at least one of the reasons supporting the need for arrest is satisfied.

2.6   Extending the power of arrest to all offences provides a constable with the ability to use that power to deal with any situation.  However applying the necessity criteria requires the constable to examine and justify the reason or reasons why a person needs to be arrested or (as the case may be) further arrested, for an offence for the custody officer to decide whether to authorise their detention for that offence.  See *Note 2C*

2.7   The criteria in paragraph 2.9 below which are set out in section 24 of PACE as substituted by section 110 of the Serious Organised Crime and Police Act 2005 <u>are</u> exhaustive.  However, the circumstances that may satisfy those criteria remain a matter for the operational discretion of individual officers.  Some examples are given to illustrate what those circumstances might be and what officers might consider when deciding whether arrest is necessary.

2.8 In considering the individual circumstances, the constable must take into account the situation of the victim, the nature of the offence, the circumstances of the suspect and the needs of the investigative process.

2.9 When it is practicable to tell a person why their arrest is necessary (as required by paragraphs 2.2, 3.3 and *Note 3*), the constable should outline the facts, information and other circumstances which provide the grounds for believing that their arrest is necessary and which the officer considers satisfy one or more of the statutory criteria in sub-paragraphs (a) to (f), namely:

(a) to enable the name of the person in question to be ascertained (in the case where the constable does not know, and cannot readily ascertain, the person's name, or has reasonable grounds for doubting whether a name given by the person as his name is his real name):

An officer might decide that a person's name cannot be readily ascertained if they fail or refuse to give it when asked, particularly after being warned that failure or refusal is likely to make their arrest necessary (see *Note 2D*). Grounds to doubt a name given may arise if the person appears reluctant or hesitant when asked to give their name or to verify the name they have given.

Where mobile fingerprinting is available and the suspect's name cannot be ascertained or is doubted, the officer should consider using the power under section 61(6A) of PACE (see *Code D paragraph 4.3(e)*) to take and check the fingerprints of a suspect as this may avoid the need to arrest solely to enable their name to be ascertained.

(b) correspondingly as regards the person's address:

An officer might decide that a person's address cannot be readily ascertained if they fail or refuse to give it when asked, particularly after being warned that such a failure or refusal is likely to make their arrest necessary. See *Note 2D*. Grounds to doubt an address given may arise if the person appears reluctant or hesitant when asked to give their address or is unable to provide verifiable details of the locality they claim to live in.

When considering reporting to consider summons or charging by post as alternatives to arrest, an address would be satisfactory if the person will be at it for a sufficiently long period for it to be possible to serve them with the summons or requisition and charge; or, that some other person at that address specified by the person will accept service on their behalf. When considering issuing a penalty notice, the address should be one where the person will be in the event of enforcement action if the person does not pay the penalty or is convicted and fined after a court hearing.

(c) to prevent the person in question:

(i) causing physical injury to himself or any other person;

This might apply where the suspect has already used or threatened violence against others and it is thought likely that they may assault others if they are not arrested. See *Note 2D*

(ii)  suffering physical injury;

This might apply where the suspect's behaviour and actions are believed likely to provoke, or have provoked, others to want to assault the suspect unless the suspect is arrested for their own protection.  See *Note 2D*

(iii) causing loss or damage to property;

This might apply where the suspect is a known persistent offender with a history of serial offending against property (theft and criminal damage) and it is thought likely that they may continue offending if they are not arrested.

(iv) committing an offence against public decency (only applies where members of the public going about their normal business cannot reasonably be expected to avoid the person in question);

This might apply when an offence against public decency is being committed in a place to which the public have access and is likely to be repeated in that or some other public place at a time when the public are likely to encounter the suspect.  See *Note 2D*

(v)  causing an unlawful obstruction of the highway;

This might apply to any offence where its commission causes an unlawful obstruction which it is believed may continue or be repeated if the person is not arrested, particularly if the person has been warned that they are causing an obstruction.  See *Note 2D*

(d) to protect a child or other vulnerable person from the person in question.

This might apply when the health (physical or mental) or welfare of a child or vulnerable person is likely to be harmed or is at risk of being harmed, if the person is not arrested in cases where it is not practicable and appropriate to make alternative arrangements to prevent the suspect from having any harmful or potentially harmful contact with the child or vulnerable person.

(e) to allow the prompt and effective investigation of the offence or of the conduct of the person in question.  See *Note 2E*

This may arise when it is thought likely that unless the person is arrested and then either taken in custody to the police station or granted 'street bail' to attend the station later, see *Note 2J*, further action considered necessary to properly investigate their involvement in the offence would be frustrated, unreasonably delayed or otherwise hindered and therefore be impracticable.  Examples of such actions include:

*(i)  interviewing the suspect* on occasions when the person's voluntary attendance is not considered to be a practicable alternative to arrest, because for example:

- it is thought unlikely that the person would attend the police station voluntarily to be interviewed.
- it is necessary to interview the suspect about the outcome of other investigative action for which their arrest is necessary, see (ii) to (v) below.

- arrest would enable the special warning to be given in accordance with Code C paragraphs 10.10 and 10.11 when the suspect is found:
  - ~ in possession of incriminating objects, or at a place where such objects are found;
  - ~ at or near the scene of the crime at or about the time it was committed.
- the person has made false statements and/or presented false evidence;
- it is thought likely that the person:
  - ~ may steal or destroy evidence;
  - ~ may collude or make contact with, co-suspects or conspirators;
  - ~ may intimidate or threaten or make contact with, witnesses.

See *Notes 2F and 2G*

(ii) when considering arrest in connection with the investigation of an *indictable offence* (see *Note 6*), there is a need:

- to enter and search without a search warrant any premises occupied or controlled by the arrested person or where the person was when arrested or immediately before arrest;
- to prevent the arrested person from having contact with others;
- to detain the arrested person for more than 24 hours before charge.

(iii) when considering arrest in connection with any *recordable offence* and it is necessary to secure or preserve evidence of that offence by taking fingerprints, footwear impressions or samples from the suspect for evidential comparison or matching with other material relating to that offence, for example, from the crime scene. See *Note 2H*

(iv) when considering arrest in connection with any offence and it is necessary to search, examine or photograph the person to obtain evidence. See *Note 2H*

(v) when considering arrest in connection with an offence to which the statutory Class A drug testing requirements in Code C section 17 apply, to enable testing when it is thought that drug misuse might have caused or contributed to the offence. See *Note 2I*.

(f) to prevent any prosecution for the offence from being hindered by the disappearance of the person in question.

This may arise when it is thought that:

- if the person is not arrested they are unlikely to attend court if they are prosecuted;
- the address given is not a satisfactory address for service of a summons or a written charge and requisition to appear at court because the person will not be at it for a sufficiently long period for the summons or charge and requisition to be served and no other person at that specified address will accept service on their behalf.

## 3 Information to be given on Arrest

### *(a) Cautions - when a caution must be given*

3.1 Code C paragraphs 10.1 and 10.2 set out the requirement for a person whom there are grounds to suspect of an offence (see *Note 2*) to be cautioned before being questioned or further questioned about an offence.

3.2 *Not used.*

3.3 A person who is arrested, or further arrested, must be informed at the time if practicable, or if not, as soon as it becomes practicable thereafter, that they are under arrest and of the grounds and reasons for their arrest, see paragraphs 2.2 and *Note 3*.

3.4 A person who is arrested, or further arrested, must be cautioned unless:

   (a) it is impracticable to do so by reason of their condition or behaviour at the time;

   (b) they have already been cautioned immediately prior to arrest as in *paragraph 3.1*.

### *(b) Terms of the caution (Taken from Code C section 10)*

3.5 The caution, which must be given on arrest, should be in the following terms:

"You do not have to say anything.  But it may harm your defence if you do not mention when questioned something which you later rely on in Court. Anything you do say may be given in evidence."

Where the use of the Welsh Language is appropriate, a constable may provide the caution directly in Welsh in the following terms:

*"Does dim rhaid i chi ddweud dim byd. Ond gall niweidio eich amddiffyniad os na fyddwch chi'n sôn, wrth gael eich holi, am rywbeth y byddwch chi'n dibynnu arno nes ymlaen yn y Llys. Gall unrhyw beth yr ydych yn ei ddweud gael ei roi fel tystiolaeth."*

See *Note 4*

3.6 Minor deviations from the words of any caution given in accordance with this Code do not constitute a breach of this Code, provided the sense of the relevant caution is preserved.  See *Note 5*

3.7 *Not used.*

## 4 Records of Arrest

### *(a) General*

4.1 The arresting officer is required to record in his pocket book or by other methods used for recording information:

- the nature and circumstances of the offence leading to the arrest;
- the reason or reasons why arrest was necessary;
- the giving of the caution; and
- anything said by the person at the time of arrest.

4.2     Such a record should be made at the time of the arrest unless impracticable to do.  If not made at that time, the record should then be completed as soon as possible thereafter.

4.3     On arrival at the police station or after being first arrested at the police station, the arrested person must be brought before the custody officer as soon as practicable and a custody record must be opened in accordance with section 2 of Code C.  The information given by the arresting officer on the circumstances and reason or reasons for arrest shall be recorded as part of the custody record.  Alternatively, a copy of the record made by the officer in accordance with paragraph 4.1 above shall be attached as part of the custody record.  See *paragraph 2.2* and *Code C paragraphs 3.4* and *10.3.*

4.4     The custody record will serve as a record of the arrest.  Copies of the custody record will be provided in accordance with paragraphs 2.4 and 2.4A of Code C and access for inspection of the original record in accordance with paragraph 2.5 of Code C.

### (b) Interviews and arrests

4.5     Records of interview, significant statements or silences will be treated in the same way as set out in sections 10 and 11 of Code C and in Codes E and F (audio and visual recording of interviews).

### Notes for Guidance

1       *For the purposes of this Code, 'offence' means any statutory or common law offence for which a person may be tried by a magistrates' court or the Crown court and punished if convicted.  Statutory offences include assault, rape, criminal damage, theft, robbery, burglary, fraud, possession of controlled drugs and offences under road traffic, liquor licensing, gambling and immigration legislation and local government byelaws.  Common law offences include murder, manslaughter, kidnapping, false imprisonment, perverting the course of justice and escape from lawful custody.*

1A      *This code does not apply to powers of arrest conferred on constables under any arrest warrant, for example, a warrant issued under the Magistrates' Courts Act 1980, sections 1 or 13, or the Bail Act 1976, section 7(1), or to the powers of constables to arrest without warrant other than under section 24 of PACE for an offence.  These other powers to arrest without warrant do not depend on the arrested person committing any specific offence and include:*

- *PACE, section 46A, arrest of person who fails to answer police bail to attend police station or is suspected of breaching any condition of that bail for the custody officer to decide whether they should be kept in police detention which applies whether or not the person commits an offence under section 6 of the Bail Act 1976 (e.g. failing without reasonable cause to surrender to custody);*

- *Bail Act 1976, section 7(3), arrest of person bailed to attend court who is suspected of breaching, or is believed likely to breach, any condition of bail to take them to court for bail to be re-considered;*

- *Children & Young Persons Act 1969, section 32(1A) (absconding) - arrest to return the person to the place where they are required to reside;*

- *Immigration Act 1971, Schedule 2 to arrest a person liable to examination to determine their right to remain in the UK;*

- *Mental Health Act 1983, section 136 to remove person suffering from mental disorder to place of safety for assessment;*

- *Prison Act 1952, section 49, arrest to return person unlawfully at large to the prison etc. where they are liable to be detained;*

- *Road Traffic Act 1988, section 6D arrest of driver following the outcome of a preliminary roadside test requirement to enable the driver to be required to provide an evidential sample;*

- *Common law power to stop or prevent a Breach of the Peace - after arrest a person aged 18 or over may be brought before a justice of the peace court to show cause why they should not be bound over to keep the peace - not criminal proceedings.*

1B    *Juveniles should not be arrested at their place of education unless this is unavoidable.  When a juvenile is arrested at their place of education, the principal or their nominee must be informed.  (From Code C Note 11D)*

2    *Facts and information relevant to a person's suspected involvement in an offence should not be confined to those which tend to indicate the person has committed or attempted to commit the offence.  Before making a decision to arrest, a constable should take account of any facts and information that are available, including claims of innocence made by the person, that might dispel the suspicion.*

2A    *Particular examples of facts and information which might point to a person's innocence and may tend to dispel suspicion include those which relate to the statutory defence provided by the Criminal Law Act 1967, section 3(1) which allows the use of reasonable force in the prevention of crime or making an arrest and the common law of self-defence.  This may be relevant when a person appears, or claims, to have been acting reasonably in defence of themselves or others or to prevent their property or the property of others from being stolen, destroyed or damaged, particularly if the offence alleged is based on the use of unlawful force, e.g. a criminal assault.  When investigating allegations involving the use of force by school staff, the power given to all school staff under the Education and Inspections Act 2006, section 93, to use reasonable force to prevent their pupils from committing any offence, injuring persons, damaging property or prejudicing the maintenance of good order and discipline may be similarly relevant.  The Association of Chief Police Officers and the Crown Prosecution Service have published joint guidance to help the public understand the meaning of reasonable force and what to expect from the police and CPS in cases which involve claims of self defence.  Separate advice for school staff on their powers to use reasonable force is available from the Department for Education*

2B    *If a constable who is dealing with an allegation of crime and considering the need to arrest becomes an investigator for the purposes of the Code of Practice under the Criminal Procedure and Investigations Act 1996, the officer should, in accordance with paragraph 3.5 of that Code, "pursue all reasonable lines of inquiry, whether these point towards or away from the suspect.  What is reasonable in each case will depend on the particular circumstances."*

2C    *For a constable to have reasonable grounds for believing it necessary to arrest, he or she is not required to be satisfied that there is no viable alternative to arrest. However, it does mean that in all cases, the officer should consider that arrest is the practical, sensible and proportionate option in all the circumstances at the time the decision is made. This applies equally to a person in police detention after being arrested for an offence who is suspected of involvement in a further offence and the necessity to arrest them for that further offence is being considered.*

2D    *Although a warning is not expressly required, officers should if practicable, consider whether a warning which points out their offending behaviour, and explains why, if they do not stop, the resulting consequences may make their arrest necessary. Such a warning might:*

- *if heeded, avoid the need to arrest, or*

- *if it is ignored, support the need to arrest and also help prove the mental element of certain offences, for example, the person's intent or awareness, or help to rebut a defence that they were acting reasonably.*

*A person who is warned that they may be liable to arrest if their real name and address cannot be ascertained, should be given a reasonable opportunity to establish their real name and address before deciding that either or both are unknown and cannot be readily ascertained or that there are reasonable grounds to doubt that a name and address they have given is their real name and address. They should be told why their name is not known and cannot be readily ascertained and (as the case may be) of the grounds for doubting that a name and address they have given is their real name and address, including, for example, the reason why a particular document the person has produced to verify their real name and/or address, is not sufficient.*

2E    *The meaning of "prompt" should be considered on a case by case basis taking account of all the circumstances. It indicates that the progress of the investigation should not be delayed to the extent that it would adversely affect the effectiveness of the investigation. The arresting officer also has discretion to release the arrested person on 'street bail' as an alternative to taking the person directly to the station. See Note 2J.*

2F    *An officer who believes that it is necessary to interview the person suspected of committing the offence must then consider whether their arrest is necessary in order to carry out the interview. The officer is not required to interrogate the suspect to determine whether they will attend a police station voluntarily to be interviewed but they must consider whether the suspect's voluntary attendance is a practicable alternative for carrying out the interview. If it is, then arrest would not be necessary. Conversely, an officer who considers this option but is not satisfied that it is a practicable alternative, may have reasonable grounds for deciding that the arrest is necessary at the outset 'on the street'. Without such considerations, the officer would not be able to establish that arrest was necessary in order to interview.*

*Circumstances which suggest that a person's arrest 'on the street' would not be necessary to interview them might be where the officer:*

- *is satisfied as to their identity and address and that they will attend the police station voluntarily to be interviewed, either immediately or by arrangement at a future date and time; and*

- *is not aware of any other circumstances which indicate that voluntary attendance would not be a practicable alternative. See paragraph 2.9(e)(i) to (v).*

*When making arrangements for the person's voluntary attendance, the officer should tell the person:*

- *that to properly investigate their suspected involvement in the offence they must be interviewed under caution at the police station, but in the circumstances their arrest for this purpose will not be necessary if they attend the police station voluntarily to be interviewed;*

- *that if they attend voluntarily, they will be entitled to free legal advice before, and to have a solicitor present at, the interview;*

- *that the date and time of the interview will take account of their circumstances and the needs of the investigation; and*

- *that if they do not agree to attend voluntarily at a time which meets the needs of the investigation, or having so agreed, fail to attend, or having attended, fail to remain for the interview to be completed, their arrest will be necessary to enable them to be interviewed.*

2G    *When the person attends the police station voluntarily for interview by arrangement as in Note 2F above, their arrest on arrival at the station prior to interview would only be justified if:*

- *new information coming to light after the arrangements were made indicates that from that time, voluntary attendance ceased to be a practicable alternative and the person's arrest became necessary; and*

- *it was not reasonably practicable for the person to be arrested before they attended the station.*

*If a person who attends the police station voluntarily to be interviewed decides to leave before the interview is complete, the police would at that point be entitled to consider whether their arrest was necessary to carry out the interview. The possibility that the person might decide to leave during the interview is therefore not a valid reason for arresting them before the interview has commenced. See Code C paragraph 3.21.*

2H    *The necessity criteria do not permit arrest solely to enable the routine taking, checking (speculative searching) and retention of fingerprints, samples, footwear impressions and photographs when there are no prior grounds to believe that checking and comparing the fingerprints etc. or taking a photograph would provide relevant evidence of the person's involvement in the offence concerned or would help to ascertain or verify their real identity.*

2I      *The necessity criteria do not permit arrest for an offence solely because it happens to be one of the statutory drug testing "trigger offences" (see Code C Note 17E) when there is no suspicion that Class A drug misuse might have caused or contributed to the offence.*

2J      *Having determined that the necessity criteria have been met and having made the arrest, the officer can then consider the use of street bail on the basis of the effective and efficient progress of the investigation of the offence in question.  It gives the officer discretion to compel the person to attend a police station at a date/time that best suits the overall needs of the particular investigation.  Its use is not confined to dealing with child care issues or allowing officers to attend to more urgent operational duties and granting street bail does not retrospectively negate the need to arrest.*

3       *An arrested person must be given sufficient information to enable them to understand they have been deprived of their liberty and the reason they have been arrested, as soon as practicable after the arrest, e.g. when a person is arrested on suspicion of committing an offence they must be informed of the nature of the suspected offence and when and where it was committed.  The suspect must also be informed of the reason or reasons why arrest is considered necessary.  Vague or technical language should be avoided.  When explaining why one or more of the arrest criteria apply, it is not necessary to disclose any specific details that might undermine or otherwise adversely affect any investigative processes.  An example might be the conduct of a formal interview when prior disclosure of such details might give the suspect an opportunity to fabricate an innocent explanation or to otherwise conceal lies from the interviewer.*

4       *Nothing in this Code requires a caution to be given or repeated when informing a person not under arrest they may be prosecuted for an offence. However, a court will not be able to draw any inferences under the Criminal Justice and Public Order Act 1994, section 34, if the person was not cautioned.*

5       *If it appears a person does not understand the caution, the person giving it should explain it in their own words.*

6       *Certain powers available as the result of an arrest - for example, entry and search of premises, detention without charge beyond 24 hours, holding a person incommunicado and delaying access to legal advice -only apply in respect of indictable offences <u>and</u> are subject to the specific requirements on authorisation as set out in PACE and the relevant Code of Practice.*

YOUR NOTES

9 798885 590945